WRITE
CLEAR EMAILS

PARAG CHITNIS

Clever Fox® PUBLISHING

Chennai • Bangalore

CLEVER FOX PUBLISHING
Chennai, India

Published by CLEVER FOX PUBLISHING 2025

ISBN: 978-93-6707-370-4

CONTENTS

LET'S START

Let's read some emails

It was a bright and sunny morning at the operations headquarters. For the customer support team, the day began like any other. Little did they know that a storm was about to break and they were right in its path.

From: Customer
To: Customer Support Team
Subject: Website Launch Delay

Team
I am told that yesterday's launch didn't go through. This is disappointing. What happened?

Regards,
Arvind Joshi

From: Customer Support Executive
To: Customer
Subject: Re: Website Launch Delay

Arvind
Thank you for your email. First of all, I would like to say that we are really very sorry for the delay in the launch, but it was beyond our control. The day before yesterday, we were ready for launch, but just yesterday at the last minute, there were some unexpected hiccups, so we are working on the new date. The vendor wanted more testing; we told him about the launch date, but he kept insisting on it, so we delayed the launch. We hope to complete the testing in the next three days or so, and we immensely appreciate your patience. Thank you. Have a great day.

Regards,
The Customer Support Team

From: Customer
To: Customer Support Team
Subject: Re: Website Launch Delay

What's that supposed to mean? And what do you mean by 'you hope to'? This is unacceptable.

Arvind Joshi

From: Senior Support Manager
To: Customer
Subject: Re: Website Launch Delay

Dear Arvind,
I understand your frustration and appreciate your patience. Let me clarify the situation.

We delayed the launch because of an issue with the payment gateway. Yesterday evening, the security vendor discovered a vulnerability that would have compromised customer data. I'm attaching a detailed report. Rushing to launch would have degraded customer experience, and we know how much you value your customers.

We have fixed the problem, and testing has started. The revised launch date is May 15. I'll keep you posted with daily updates.

I apologize for the delay and assure you that we are working to deliver a superior product. Thank you for your understanding and continued partnership.

Sincerely,
Raj Shah

From: Customer
To: Customer Support Team
Subject: Re: Website Launch Delay

Dear Raj,
Thank you for the explanation. I understand the necessity behind the delay and agree with the decision. I look forward to a successful launch.

Regards,
Arvind

Why write clear emails?

The customer support team weathered the storm, thanks to Raj's timely intervention. A clear and well-written email helped save the day. It diffused the situation and regained the customer's confidence.

Good communication is the backbone of every business. In a world where business decisions hinge on written exchanges, clear emails can be the difference between success and failure.

Save your job

Emails are a constant but rarely acknowledged form of evaluation. Every message you send shapes how others see you, mostly at a subconscious level. Your manager may not tell you that he hates your emails, but the sentiment will eventually reflect in your appraisal.

In today's CC culture, where senior leaders are looped in on every other email, your writing shapes their first impression of you. You don't want their impression to be, "What's this moron trying to say?"

Save your time

When your message is easy to understand, you avoid endless back-and-forth and needless calls to clarify what you meant. That means less time spent on follow-ups and more time on actual work.

Build credibility

When people consistently understand your emails the first time, they begin to see you as someone who's reliable and capable. They are more likely to act on your inputs and seek your opinion.

Every word you write shapes how others see you. A well-written email demonstrates respect, professionalism, and competence, whereas a careless one can come across as rude, unprofessional, or outright incompetent.

Establish authority

Whether you're explaining a plan, responding to a concern, or making a request, a well-written email gives your message weight and earns you the recognition of your peers. Over time, this reinforces your authority and establishes your brand.

Develop a professional edge

Good writing brings clarity, builds confidence, and drives action. Bad writing creates doubt, spreads confusion, and halts progress. In today's competitive workplaces, clarity isn't a luxury—it's a professional edge.

What is clarity?

Why do we write emails? We write emails so that someone can read them. The purpose of an email is to be read and understood. Understanding is the truest test of an email, and the responsibility rests solely on the writer's shoulders.

Clarity is when your reader

- Understands what you wrote.
- Understands it quickly.
- Understands it without effort.
- Does not misunderstand.
- Does not have questions or doubts.

Clarity means getting to the point quickly without making the reader work for it. A clear email keeps the reader focused and doesn't let him get distracted. It's a straight line, not a complex maze. Clarity is about getting your message across the first time, every time.

Clarity is the difference between being understood and being ignored. Clarity is the difference between being a somebody and a nobody. Clarity is what sets you apart from the crowd.

Elements of a clear email

To write a clear email, you must know the answer to these five questions.

1. Who am I writing to?
2. What do I want them to know?
3. What do I want them to do?
4. Why is it important?
5. When do I want it done?

Who am I writing to?

Which of these is a better way of inviting a friend to a party?

1. You stand beneath his building and shout out the invitation at the top of your voice, or
2. You ring his doorbell and tell him personally.

You don't need rockstar social skills to know the answer. The same applies to emails.

Don't send an email to a team alias with twenty engineers, two team leads, and one manager, and hope that the correct person responds. Put his email ID in the 'To' section of your email. The team alias can go in CC.

Start the email by addressing the person you are writing to. Let everyone know who the main recipient of your email is. Start with 'Dear Jay', and not 'Dear Team'.

If you don't know who does what in a particular team, make some inquires beforehand. At least find out who heads the team and address them in your email, and ask them for a point of contact for the topic of your email.

What do I want them to know?

Imagine you are sending an invitation for a team meeting. Would you rather say, "Hey, let's meet", or would you rather tell them, "Let's meet to take a decision, or brainstorm, or get a status update." You don't want ten people to gather in the conference room and discuss the new coffee machine, do you?

Purpose and clarity are inseparable. You cannot write a clear email without being clear about what you want to say. Start by telling yourself what you want to tell others.

A simple trick is to finish this sentence.

> I want the reader to know that ____________________.
>
> I want the reader to know that <u>I have submitted the proposal</u>.
> I want the reader to know that <u>I need her help</u>.
> I want the reader to know that <u>the customer is angry</u>.

If you feel the need to go beyond one line or one point, use a point-wise template.

> I want my reader to know the following –
> 1. The software has crashed.
> 2. The customer is angry.
> 3. He demands a resolution in 24 hours.

What do I want the reader to do?

Rarely do we write an email merely for the sake of informing someone: "Hey, I thought of sharing this with you, but you don't need to do anything about it." Most emails are written with the expectation of an action. Make the action explicitly clear.

Tell the reader clearly what you want him to do. Don't assume that it is obvious. Spell it out. Get specific.

I want the reader to __________________.

I want the reader to draft a one-page root cause document.
I want the reader to fix bug no. HF-482.
I want the reader to come to the meeting with a 5-slide presentation.

Leave no room for doubt about what needs to happen and who must do it. If there are multiple actions, list them down using numbers. If different people are supposed to take different actions, then put their names next to each action.

Why is it important?

A teacher and his disciple were walking through a forest when they came upon a river. The river seemed shallow enough to cross, so they decided to wade through. As they were about to step into the water, the teacher paused. "Keep your shoes on as you cross," he advised the disciple.

The disciple looked down at his new shoes and decided he didn't want to spoil them. He removed them and walked barefoot into the cool stream, unaware of the sharp stones lurking beneath. With every step, the stones cut through his feet, and he emerged on the other side, feet bleeding and limping.

"Why didn't you warn me that I'd cut my feet?" he screamed at his teacher in pain. The teacher's eyes crinkled in a gentle smile as he replied, "Because life gives lessons first, and explains later."

You are sending an email, not giving life lessons. Tell people why you want them to do something. Tell them why it is important. Help them understand the consequences of inaction. Only then will they act upon it.

When do I want it done?

ASAP stands for "as soon as possible", and not urgently. If you want it done urgently, say urgently. But that's not enough. How urgent is urgently—1 day, 1 hour, 1 minute. Give people a clear timeline. Don't expect them to read your mind or understand the urgency of the situation.

Vague: Let's talk soon.
Clear: Let's talk tomorrow at 10 am.

Vague: Get it done quickly.
Clear: We need to submit it by 12 pm Thursday. So, please complete it by 3 pm, Wednesday so that I have time to review it.

Vague: EOD, COB
Clear: 6 pm, today

Confusing: The meeting will happen next Wednesday.

Which Wednesday is that? The coming Wednesday or the one after?

Clear: The meeting will happen on Wednesday, 12th June.

In a global workplace, sometimes even clear may not be enough—you must be precise.

Clear but not enough: 5th September, 12 pm

Precise: 5th September, 12 pm, IST

Use the elements as a guiding light to create clear and to-the-point emails. Don't treat them like a rigid checklist because not every email will need every element. Instead, think of them as tools in a toolbox—use only the ones that best fit the task.

This book isn't about prescribing a formula. It's about giving you the right tools. The key is to apply your judgment. Writing well is not about ticking boxes. It's about communicating effectively. Let the elements guide you, not blind you.

Let's write a clear email

Let's create an email using these 5 elements. We'll start by gathering information. You can do it in your head or jot it down somewhere.

1. **I'm writing to** Jas from Engineering.
2. **I want him to know that** –
   a. The checkout page is not loading.
   b. The client is upset about it.
3. **I want him to do the following** –
   a. Investigate and find the cause of the problem.
   b. Submit a one-page root cause analysis.
   c. Tell me when he will fix the issue.
4. **This is important because** the bug is blocking the website launch, which opens us up to penalties.
5. **This needs to happen before** 25 March.

Now, let's convert this information into an email. Take a pen and paper and try doing it by yourself. Then, turn the page and compare it with what I have written.

Here's how I have written it:

To: Jas
CC: Engineering

Subject: Launch blocker – Resolution needed

Hi Jas,

The checkout page is not working, and the client is upset about it. Can you please look into this urgently? I need you to do the following –

1. Investigate the problem.
2. Submit a one-page root cause analysis.
3. Commit to a resolution date.

This is important because it's blocking the website launch and opens us up to penalties. So please complete the requested activities and get back to me by 25th March, 5 pm.

Regards,
Ria

The email you have written doesn't have to match what I have written. What matters is that you have covered all the points that we had listed.

STRUCTURE

Subject

The subject line is the first thing your recipient sees. It can determine whether your email is opened or overlooked. A clear, concise, and direct subject line increases the chances that your email is read promptly.

Remember to write the subject line. Nothing feels more foolish than replying to your own email with 8 people in To and 24 in CC, and saying:

Sorry. I had forgotten to put the subject.

Let your subject line stand out, but don't make it scream. Avoid subject lines written entirely in uppercase. An occasional IMPORTANT, URGENT, or CRITICAL prefix is okay, but don't make it a habit. It will stop feeling important.

Your recipient will see around 6 words of the subject on a mobile and 8-10 on a laptop. If you ignore words like of, to, for and in, you are left with 3-4 keywords to grab attention with. Choose them carefully.

> **Too long:** Please submit your timesheet tomorrow without fail
> **To the point:** Timesheet due tomorrow

Use keywords that stand out.

> **Vague:** Q2 Budget
> **Specific:** Approval needed – Q2 Budget

The best subject lines provide just enough information so that the reader doesn't need to dig into the content. Be specific. Include date or time wherever applicable.

Vague: Meeting updated
Specific: Ops Meeting rescheduled to 5 pm

If the email revolves around an action, make the action clear in the subject itself.

Unclear action: Draft Report
Clear action: Draft Report for review

Make full use of the subject line, but remember to keep it short, concise, and relevant.

Salutation and Sign-off

Set the right tone

The first line of an email sets the tone for the rest of the message. It is respectful to start the email by addressing the person you are writing to. Omitting the salutation can make your message sound curt and make your readers feel invisible.

Choose wisely

Choose the right salutation based on company etiquette and your relationship with the recipient. It's okay to say Dear, Hi, Hello or simply the name. Avoid the causal sounding Hey, unless you are close friends and it's acceptable in your work culture.

Use professional titles where appropriate: Dr. for doctors, and rank for military personnel. When using Mr., Mrs., or Ms., be mindful of the recipient's gender and marriage status. When in doubt, use Dear.

End on the right note

Emails without a sign-off can make the reader feel ghosted—as if you vanished mid-conversation. When signing off, stick to your company norm. Regards, Sincerely or Thank you, they all work well.

Skip the temperature settings on your regards. Don't send Warm or Best Regards unless you also send cold or worst regards. Be mindful of preset email signatures—keep them neutral.

Be sensitive. Ending an email about working late with "Have a great day" can make you sound like a jerk, and wrapping up a stern message with "Cheers" can undermine its seriousness.

Long emails? Think again

Write short emails. People open an email expecting one or two paragraphs. They don't want a 600-word essay. They will shut their laptop and go for coffee.

If your email is longer than five paragraphs, think again.

- Can you shorten it?
- Are all points related?
- Even if they are, do they need to be in the same email?

If the topic is the same but the message varies by team, break it into different emails. Send a common email to everyone, and follow it with targeted emails to specific groups.

Check if there are parts of your message that can be sent as an attachment. This keeps your message concise while still making all the details available.

Finally, if you must write a long email, spend enough time structuring it.

- Use paragraphs judiciously.
- Give enough headings at key places.
- Highlight or emphasize important text.

Long emails are a burden on memory. People forget the beginning and middle by the time they reach the end. So, remember to include a brief conclusion with key takeaways.

Paragraphs

Let your readers breathe

A long unbroken stream of text can leave the reader gasping for breath. Dumping all your thoughts into one big block makes your writing look shabby and disorganized. It comes across as hastily written, with little thought behind it.

Organize your content into paragraphs, each carrying one chain of thought. If a thought is too big, break it into multiple paragraphs. Keep the paragraphs short and evenly sized. Maintain a consistent size, but don't be rigid about it.

Make it readable

Paragraphs improve the readability of your content. Readability helps people navigate through multiple ideas without getting lost or feeling overwhelmed by their size. The space between two paragraphs gives your readers a chance to pause and absorb what you have written.

When creating paragraphs, introduce ideas such that one thought leads to another. Start with the context, follow it up with details, and end it with an action or a conclusion. Don't switch between two points. It makes the reader look back and forth. Complete one point before moving to the next.

Your emails are often the first impression you make, and they reflect your personality more than you realize. Use paragraphs not just for structure, but to show that you're organized in your thinking. A well-formatted email doesn't just convey information. It shows thoughtfulness and focus.

Make it look good

People appreciate beauty

The human brain is designed to appreciate and trust beauty. Whether it's a smartly dressed person or a neatly organized email, aesthetics matter. They play a crucial role in how people read and respond to your email.

A well-structured and good-looking email feels easier to read and sounds more compelling. A poorly structured email, on the other hand, can come across as rushed or careless, no matter how good the content.

Be consistent

An email cluttered with large blocks of text in different fonts and sizes is a pain to read.

- Choose a medium-size and formal-looking font.
- Use minimal colours. Black works most of the time.
- Remember to format externally copy-pasted text.

Numbers and bullet points

A dense block of text slows people down and increases the chance of missing key points. A long explanation like the one below is hard to understand. People may skim through it and miss important points, or worse, ignore it completely.

Here is an example:

As part of its processing, the software first parses the query, extracts keys from it, then queries the primary database, then the secondary database, then it compares both results, chooses the more recent record, and then returns the record back to the client.

Consider using a numbered or a bullet-point list.

This is how the software processes a query.

1. Parses the query
2. Extracts keys
3. Queries the primary database
4. Queries the secondary database
5. Returns the more recent record to the client

Numbers, bullets, and headings help the reader navigate your email without having to read it again and again.

- Use bullets when you are presenting connected ideas, but need each point to stand out.
- Use numbers to show a sequence or an order of preference.

Emphasize, but don't shout

Give emphasis and headings wherever necessary.

- Use bold text for emphasis
- Change colour to highlight key points.
- Add headings to separate different sections
- Use indentation to show hierarchy.

But don't overdo it. If you emphasize everything, nothing will stand out.

Double-check your spelling

Don't be ashamed of using spell checks. Nothing tanks credibility faster than a misspelled word. And misspelling someone's name? That's just insulting. You might as well tell them that they're worthless.

Keep related things together

Keep images and related text one below the other. Show an image and then explain it. Don't make the reader open an attachment and then switch between the image and its text.

Be careful with images

Images can resize differently across browsers and devices, disrupting the layout. If you use images, first test them by sending the email to a trusted colleague.

Value your reader's time

When sharing results or analysis, start with a concise summary that highlights the key conclusion, and include the detailed document as an attachment. Don't send an email saying PFA and attach a 20-page report.

Take it seriously

How you present your emails is part of your professional identity. It's a subtle signal to others that you take your work seriously and hence are worth listening to. Show your readers that the email matters to you, and so do they.

SENTENCES

Keep it short

Read this sentence.

> As the first light of day gently pierced the horizon, the golden orb in the sky began its majestic ascent, casting its warm and amber glow across the slumbering earth, turning everything it touched into a shimmering tapestry of radiant hues, bathing the world in its soft, ethereal brilliance.

Did you finish the sentence, or did you give up halfway? Next, did you understand it? Lastly, once you understood it, did you feel like punching me? Now, let's say the same thing in a different way.

> The sun rose.

You are writing an email, not a novel. The goal is to make a point, not celebrate the English language. People might want their novels vibrant and colourful, but they prefer their emails plain and clear.

Use short sentences

Stop writing after 15 words. Rarely go past 18 words. Never exceed 22 words. If you have more to say, break it into two sentences. Think of it like eating—you can only eat so much in one bite. Anything more, your reader will choke.

Let every sentence convey one clear point. Most people can grasp and retain only one thing at a time. If you cram multiple ideas into a single sentence, a few will get lost.

Lesser the better

Prominent editor and journalist, Harold Evans, makes a strong case for to-the-point writing in his book *Essential English for Journalists, Editors and Writers.*[1] He gives an example of a fishmonger who has a sign over his shop:

FRESH FISH SOLD HERE

A friend notices the sign and suggests trimming it down. He first persuades the fishmonger to erase the word FRESH—because who would sell stale fish? Next, he gets rid of the word HERE, because naturally, he is selling it here in the shop.

By now, the friend is on a roll. He soon gets rid of the word SOLD—obviously; the fish is being sold and not given away for free. And lastly, we are left with a blank sign as he erases the word FISH, because of course it's fish, you can smell it a mile away.

Don't send blank emails, but do cut all unnecessary words from your message. Let's use the sentence below as a case study.

We are presently in the process of creation of the plan of action.

Sure, it's correct, but it's carrying too much verbal baggage. Let's take it apart word by word and shorten it without losing its meaning or spirit.

Let's start with *presently.* It is redundant because, unless you say otherwise, everything is in the present. Let's scratch it off.

We are in the process of creation of the plan of action.

Next on our radar is *creation of.* It sounds needlessly formal and heavy. Let's change it to *creating.*

We are in the process of creating the plan of action.

Next in our plan is *the plan of action.* Is it *a plan* or *the plan*? Unless you are writing about the mother of all plans, it is *a plan.* Also, every plan is about doing something, even if that something happens to be nothing. So, it's sufficient to say plan.

We are in the process of creating a plan.

That leaves us with four words you can always get rid of: in the process of. The meaning will remain unchanged.

We are creating a plan.

You can stop here, but I urge you to continue. Let's take another look at the word *creating*. God *created* this earth. People like you and me, we *make* plans. So, we change it to:

We are making a plan.

If making a plan is too bland for your taste, you can go with:

We are putting together a plan.

We just shortened a sentence from 13 words to 5—a reduction of 61.5%. Consider how many people read your emails every day.

Now imagine the time your company could save if each of those emails were just a little shorter and more direct.

Counting your words and then trimming them is a simple but powerful technique. It may sound obvious, yet it's something we rarely do in practice. I came across this idea in Harold Evans' *Do I Make Myself Clear*, and it has stayed with me ever since.[2]

Now, some of you might ask, "What about *making a plan*? Why not shorten it as well?" Well, let's try shortening it.

We are planning.

Sure, it's short, but the sentence feels somewhat incomplete. This is where you must use your judgment. I see two choices: you can go back to the previous version, or you can add a few words to describe what you are planning.

We are planning the next software release.

Remember, every idea in this book is a tool meant to help you convey your thoughts clearly. These are not rules set in stone. Use them until they make sense, and stop when they don't.

Right now, it's time for a quick check-in.

Your turn

It's your turn. Take a pen and paper, and try shortening this sentence.

> In order to ensure that the team was very well-prepared for the upcoming project, a series of sessions were organized and conducted by us in which they were trained on the product that they were going to work on.

As you work on it, remember this:

- There are no right or wrong answers. There is always more than one way to achieve clarity.
- Each of us will approach it in our own way. What matters is finding your own words.
- Keep the meaning unchanged. After all, our main objective is to be clear, not brief.
- Do it step by step. Even I didn't get it right in one go.
- Take your time.

I'll see you on the next page.

Now that you've done it, let's find out how I did it. Here's a trick I use to shorten long sentences: divide and conquer. Break the sentence into smaller parts and work on one part at a time.

> In order to ensure that the team was very well-prepared for the upcoming project
>
> a series of sessions were organized and conducted by us
>
> in which they were trained on the product that they were going to work on.

Let's take the first part. I started by replacing *in order to* with *to.*

> To ensure that the team was very well-prepared for the upcoming project

Next was *very well-prepared.* Unless you are trying to show off, it's sufficient to say *prepared.* That leaves us with:

> To ensure that the team was prepared for the upcoming project

Let's say it in a less roundabout way:

> To prepare the team for the upcoming project

Let's proceed to part two.

> a series of sessions were organized and delivered by us

The words *a series of sessions* can be shortened to just *sessions*. Also, it is sufficient to say either *organized* or *delivered*—you don't need to say both. In fact, I chose a different variant, a lighter one: *held*.

sessions were held by us

Now, it's time for part three:

in which they were trained on the product that they were going to work on.

I simply deleted the words *that they were going to work on* because it's understood. That leaves us with:

in which they were trained on the product.

Now, let's look at all the parts together and try to stitch them together.

To prepare the team for the upcoming project sessions were held by us in which they were trained on the product.

The sentence in front of us sounds pretty awkward. So, let's rephrase it by playing a game. Imagine you're having a conversation with your readers. Tell them about the sessions and answer their questions—not by quoting the above sentence, but by explaining what it means.

You: Sessions were held by us.

Wait! That sounds odd. Let's say it differently.

You: We held some sessions.

Yes, that's better. Let's continue.

You: We held some sessions. Reader: What sessions? You: Product trainings. Reader: For whom? You: For the team, of course! Reader: But why? You: To prepare them for the upcoming project. Reader: Okay. Got it.

Now take everything you just said, and stitch it into one sentence.

We held some sessions (product trainings) for the team to prepare them for the upcoming project.

Tweak it a bit and you get:

We held product trainings to prepare the team for the upcoming project.

That's it. A 39-word sentence, shortened to 12. But let's keep going and find more ways of keeping it brief, yet clear.

Be active, not passive

Here's a line from Alfred Tennyson's poem, *The Charge of the Light Brigade*.[3]

Into the valley of death rode the six hundred.

An epic line from an immortal poem—dramatic, suspenseful, and vivid. This kind of writing suits a poem or a novel but feels off in an email. Imagine writing:

Into the meeting room everybody should assemble.

Now try:

Everybody should assemble in the meeting room.

A sentence can be written in two voices: active and passive.

Active voice: Ajay submitted the report. **Passive voice:** The report was submitted by Ajay.

Write in an active voice as much as possible. It feels more direct and natural. Think of it this way. Suppose you were directing a musical concert. Would you have your lead singer stand in front of the chorus or hide behind it? Ajay is the hero of this sentence, so put him at the beginning of the sentence.

Another reason to favor active is the way both voices sound. Active sounds confident, energetic, and decisive. It conveys a sense of ownership and control. Active sentences make the writer appear authoritative and proactive.

Passive, on the other hand, sounds slow, indirect, and lazy. It gives a sense of inaction or lack of control. It evokes images of you lounging on a recliner by the beach, not those of a person who gets things done.

Read the sentence pairs below. The active one will sound decisive, and the passive one will feel lethargic.

Active: We will achieve the quarterly targets.
Passive: The quarterly targets will be achieved by us.

Active: The team missed the deadline due to delays in receiving client feedback.
Passive: The deadline was missed by the team because of delays in receiving feedback from the client.

Does that mean you should stop writing passive sentences completely? No. If you know what you are doing, go ahead and use passive voice. But if you are not sure, then you should stick to the active voice as much as you can.

Be specific

One reason to avoid the passive voice is that it often makes you write vague and half-hearted sentences. Let's look at some examples.

A mistake was made.

Who made the mistake?

The presentation was not well-understood.

Who didn't understand my presentation?

Author Edward Johnson calls such cop-outs as pussyfooting passive. You are evading responsibility by not naming the agents of the action, leaving the readers feeling short-changed.[4][2]

Compare the below sentences:

The tender will be submitted on 20th April. Amar will submit the tender on 20th April.

The first line feels like a hope and a prayer. The second line sounds like a plan. Let's look at another example.

We will solve the problem.

Who's this mythical *we* that will solve the problem? Are you part of the we? Am I part of it? Why not tell people exactly who will solve the problem?

> I have asked the operations team to solve the problem. Rajeev Arora is in charge.

Imagine you are a tester rejecting a software release. Don't write:

> The release has been rejected because of too many bugs.

Instead, take ownership of the decision by saying:

> I'm rejecting the release because it has too many bugs.

If you aspire to lead in your career, start by owning your words and your actions. Leadership begins with taking responsibility, not just for the outcomes, but also for how you communicate.

Now that we've looked at the who, let's also look into the what.

> I'm calling a meeting to discuss the punctuality situation.

What punctuality situation?

> I'm calling a meeting to discuss why people are coming late to the office.

Don't make people guess what you're trying to say. Say it clearly. Don't leave it to inference, and certainly don't make them ask. It's a waste of their time and yours.

Here is an example:

> The software was not of an acceptable nature.

What's so unacceptable about the software? Cut the mystery and just tell people what's wrong with the software.

The software was unacceptable. It was full of bugs. Even the login page crashed a few times.

Be specific in your statements. Make it clear who is doing what, and what that is. Clarity shows accountability. It builds trust and sets the tone for clear and decisive leadership.

Avoid ambiguity

Ambiguity is the enemy of clarity because it puts the responsibility of comprehending squarely on the reader's shoulders. The Hainan Island incident between the USA and China is a classic example of ambiguous communication.

In April 2001, a US Navy plane flying over the South China Sea collided with a Chinese fighter jet. The Chinese pilot lost his life, and the US aircraft had to make an emergency landing on Chinese soil. China detained the aircraft along with its crew and demanded a full apology.

Amid escalating tensions, the United States released a statement saying it was very sorry for the death of the Chinese pilot. Beijing accepted this as a formal apology and released the crew. That's when the story took an unexpected turn. The White House responded saying, "We said we were sorry. We didn't apologize."[5]

The US *sorry* was a linguistic grey area. Sorry can be an apology or an expression of regret. You are not apologizing when you tell someone, "I am sorry for your loss." What the US truly meant, and what it implied, will forever remain shrouded in ambiguity. You, on the other hand, can do a lot better.

Here is another reply that is equally ambiguous.

Question: I was told there is an issue in the report
Reply: I didn't notice any issue.

What does that mean? Is there no issue, or there might be one, but you haven't noticed it?

A clearer reply: I checked. There is no issue in the report.

Use words that clear people's confusion, not add to their doubt. Ambiguity slows down your readers, forcing them to read one more time and finally call you to ask what you really meant.

Here are some more ambiguous statements:

Original: Vikram is mentoring Rajesh. He's climbing the ranks at an impressive pace.

Who is climbing the ranks: Vikram or Rajesh?

Rewrite: Rajesh is climbing the ranks at an impressive pace. He is being mentored by Vikram.

Original: Ajay met our CEO today. He has asked for a detailed project report.

Who wants the report: Ajay or the CEO?

Rewrite: Ajay met our CEO today. The CEO has asked for a detailed project report.

Write to communicate, not conceal. Next up, some easy ways to prevent ambiguity.

Go straight ahead

Hold your readers' hands and guide them from one point to another. Take them forward, never back and forth. If they have to stop and reread, you've lost them.

Consider this sentence:

> The marketing, sales, product, and operations teams have been assigned growth targets of 20%, 25%, 20%, and 30%, respectively.

Respectively is one word notorious for making the eyes go to-and-fro. Most readers will look back and forth to match which department has what target. It is better to say it in department–target pairs.

> The marketing team has been assigned a growth target of 20%, sales 25%, product 20%, and operations 30%.

Or, you could create a table.

These are the department-wise growth targets –

Marketing	20%
Sales	25%
Product	20%
Operations	30%

Be direct when making a point. The best way is to start by telling people what the sentence is about. Consider the following sentence:

Entering its second year, after a very shaky start, for the first time, customers are calling this a successful project.

Most people will read this sentence twice. They'll stumble through it, wondering what the sentence is about. Words will keep stacking up in their head with nothing to correlate to. It's like a movie where the hero shows up after the intermission.

They breathe a sigh of relief when they finally read the words: the project. That's when they understand what the sentence is about, but by then it's too late. Without an anchor to hold on to, they've missed what was said, and must go back for a second reading.

Now try the alternative:

The project had a shaky start, but as it enters its second year, customers are finally calling it a success.

Introduce the subject of your sentence early so that your reader knows what you are talking about.

Location Location Location

Imagine being a chef at your favourite pizza joint. Where in your kitchen would you place the pizza base, sauce, and cheese? Would you keep them close together, or would you scatter them across different corners of the kitchen? You'd of course keep them close together to make your job simpler.

In the same way, keep related words together so that the connection between them is clear. Let's look at some sentences where the connection between words is not clear.

Original: Riddled with controversy, the team has decided to delay the project.

Who is riddled with controversy, the team or the project?

Rewrite: The team has decided to delay the controversial project.

Original: The CFO enquired about the launch last week.

Did the CFO enquire last week, or did the launch happen last week?

Rewrite: Last week, the CFO enquired about the launch.

Valid choice, but you might want to start the sentence with the subject, i.e., the CFO.

The CFO enquired about the launch in last week's meeting.

Original: I noticed that the software was showing incorrect records on Friday.

Did you notice the bug on Friday, or does the software misbehave only on Friday?

Rewrite: I noticed on Friday that the software was showing incorrect records.

While the distance between related words causes confusion, the closeness between unrelated words can lead to misunderstanding. Sometimes two thoughts are not meant to be together. When placed side by side, they create the illusion that they are related when in fact they are not.

The board of directors is meeting this week. Let's talk tomorrow about rising real estate prices.

The above statement gives the impression that there is a relation between the board meeting and the proposed talk. But is that so? Well, your guess is as good as mine. If indeed both things are related, then a better way of putting it would be:

The board of directors are meeting this week. They'll ask about the rising real estate prices. So, let's discuss it tomorrow.

But if they are not related, then it's better to separate the two thoughts clearly.

Let's talk about the real estate prices tomorrow. By the way, the board of directors is meeting this week. This is just a heads up–there's nothing we need to do on that front.

Here are some more ideas that are best kept away from each other.

Confusing: He was promoted last week, and the team is now working remotely. **Clear:** He was promoted last week. Meanwhile, as decided last month, the team has started working remotely.

Confusing: The supplier changed the pricing, and we hired two new employees. **Clear:** The supplier changed the pricing. In an unrelated update, we hired two new employees.

Confusing: The weather was bad yesterday, and we received approval for the new project.

Clear: The weather was bad yesterday. On a different note, we received approval for the new project.

Misplaced words force people to read again or worse guess. On an ordinary day, they can confuse your reader. On a bad day, they could completely distort your message.

WORDS

Use the right words

An email is a bunch of words put together, but they must be the right words. The right words go beyond conveying meaning. They paint a picture in your reader's mind and bring your message to life. Use the right word for the right occasion.

Some words go together, while others don't. Let's take an example. What's a better choice of words?

- I'll finish the task, or
- I'll complete the task

It's a tough question until you read this line.

You complete a task, but you finish your meal.

Suddenly, the difference becomes clear. Consider the following lines.

I'll present the report and submit my findings. I'll submit the report and present my findings.

Both lines are correct, but the second one sounds a bit better than the first. That's because the words submit and report go well together, and so do present and findings.

Here are more examples where the sentences on the right will sound better than the ones on the left.

Sounds off	Sounds right
I've created a ticket.	I've opened a ticket.
I've opened a bug.	I've raised a bug.
I okayed the proposal.	I approved the proposal.
I did a deal.	I negotiated a deal.
I acquired experience.	I gained experience.
I learnt new skills.	I acquired new skills.
I did a mistake.	I made a mistake.

Here are more word pairs that go well together.

raise a concern	file a complaint
execute a plan	implement a suggestion
meet a deadline	give a speech
send a message	voice an opinion
close a deal	share an update
make a point	sign a contract
launch a product	take a stand
provide input	roll out an update
track progress	monitor performance
follow instructions	adhere to guidelines
set goals	define objectives
solve a problem	address a concern
face challenges	overcome obstacles
outline a plan	explain the steps
highlight a risk	mitigate an issue
delegate a task	assign responsibility
state a fact	express an opinion
offer support	extend help

Use simple words

Choose simple words over difficult ones. Pick small words over big ones. Simple words are easy to understand and quick to absorb. They won't tire your readers by making them pause and decipher.

Simplicity brings lightness to your email. Lightness is important, especially at a reading speed of one email per 30 seconds. Heavy words make the brain work harder. It saps the readers' energy, reducing their grasp of the content.

Choose familiar words over big and complicated words. Every time the eye reads 'erroneous', the brain pauses and says, "Oh, he means incorrect". Do this too often and you will exhaust your readers.

Here are some commonly used words with their simpler alternatives.

utilize – use	leverage – use
resolve – solve, fix	ascertain – find out
skeptical – not sure	obtain, procure – get, buy
rectify – fix	disseminate – share, spread
equitable – fair	expedite – speed up
transformation – change	comprehend – understand
detrimental – harmful	articulate – explain
facilitate – help	indicate – show
initiate, commence – start	mitigate – reduce, ease
conclude, terminate – end, stop	conduct – do
demonstrate – show	articulate – explain

Social media platforms often discourage the use of clickable links. That's because they want to keep the users on the platform. They know that once their users step out, it's difficult to get them back. The same applies to emails.

Don't give your readers a chance to look away from your email by using acronyms and abbreviations that they have to search on Google. If you must use an abbreviation, make sure it's one they already know. PFA and BTW will work. SHM may not work. In case you didn't know, SHM stands for 'shaking my head'.[6]

When choosing your words, aim to express, not impress.

Let verbs be verbs

In the chapter 'Lesser the better', we shortened the sentence:

We are presently in the process of creation of the plan of action.

to

We are making a plan.

We had changed *creation of* to *creating* because it felt a bit off. The reason it felt off was that *creation* is a verb disguised as a noun. When you force a verb to become a noun, you drain the energy from the action making the word feel stiff and sluggish.

Here are some nouns that become more active when used as verbs:

Verb used as a Noun	Verb
take a decision	decide
give an explanation	explain
perform an analysis	analyse
conduct an investigation	investigate
provide assistance	assist
offer a suggestion	suggest
reach a conclusion	conclude
make an improvement	improve
give an approval	approve
conduct a review	review
make an observation	observe

Verb used as a Noun	Verb
is in the need of	needs
make a recommendation	recommend
make a choice	choose
take action	act
hold a discussion	discuss
give an answer	answer
make a request	request
make a payment	pay
have a meeting	meet
make an announcement	announce
give a response	respond
perform a test	test
offer an apology	apologize
provide clarification	clarify
perform a review of	review

Use words the way they were meant to be used and they'll serve you well.

Adjectives and Adverbs

Adjectives and adverbs add fluff to your words, but no value. Think twice before using them.

Team, this is a genuine problem.

What are you hoping the team will say?

Finally, a genuine problem. We were so sick of solving fake ones.

Beware of two pitfalls when using adjectives or adverbs: redundancy and degree.

Redundancy is when the noun or verb already does the job and doesn't need another word to explain it. Here are some examples where the descriptor adds nothing useful to the word it's describing.

past experience	past history
true fact	actual reality
unexpected surprise	last minute emergency
advance planning	advance warning
final conclusion	final outcome
new beginning	end result
added bonus	free gift
sudden impulse	future plan
basic fundamentals	joint collaboration
collaborative teamwork	usual custom
regular habit	foreign imports

personal opinion	serious danger
close proximity	false rumor

Degree is when you try to amplify the effect of what you are describing. It is sufficient to say, "I am busy". You aren't going to get busier by saying, "I am extremely busy". Let's look at some examples.

heartiest congratulations	deepest condolences
most sincere condolences	deeply regret
absolutely clear	absolutely necessary
completely unanimous	completely understand
totally agree	tremendously grateful
really need	completely finish
absolutely essential	absolutely refuse
clearly explain	fully comprehend
highly recommend	excessively overestimate
fully support	strongly insist
brief moment	completely empty
completely full	totally destroy
entirely complete	wholly believe
brief summary	short summary
fully clear	utterly frustrated

You might have noticed that many of the descriptors ended with *ly*. Keep an eye on them. Whenever you feel the urge to use exactly, precisely, or thoroughly, ask yourself if you really need to.

Overuse of adjectives and adverbs creates noise without adding clarity. No wonder Stephen King once said, "I believe the road to hell is paved with adverbs."[7]

Make it easy

Most people hate reading emails. Emails are a distraction from their real job. If given a choice, they'd never even go near an inbox. But they don't have a choice, so they read. And they read with one goal: to get it over with.

People read emails faster than a speeding bullet. Your email is a mere blip on a radar full of countless other emails. It must first fight for the reader's attention and then hold on to it.

Clarity begins with ease. If you want people to read your email, make it easy to read. Which of these lines would you read year after year, at an average of 85 emails per day?

Difficult: It has just now come to my attention that there has been a total failure to adhere to the committed and designated deadline, necessitating urgent and immediate corrective action to remedy this miss from our side.
Easy: I noticed that we missed the deadline. Let's fix this quickly.

Difficult: Your expedited attention to this matter of utmost criticality of nature would be greatly appreciated in order to prevent any further delays or complications in the ongoing process of work that is happening.
Easy: Please look into this urgently.

Difficult: Pursuant to our earlier correspondence, it is evident that the current operational strategy may require a comprehensive reassessment to align with our collective collaborative objectives.
Easy: We should review our plans to work better together.

Difficult: Following a thoroughly exhaustive review of the existing data that is available to us, it has become glaringly evident that a prompt recalibration of our market engagement strategy is imperative for achieving optimal outcomes of our organizational endeavours.
Easy: We've reviewed the data. We must change our market strategy right away.

Make your emails easy to read and people won't mind reading them.

Be Positive

Let's play a little mind game. I want you to try, and not to think of a white bear. Chances are that the first thing that popped into mind was a polar bear. That's how our brain works. When you tell someone not to do something, it often makes that thought stronger.[8]

Asking someone to be on time is more likely to keep them punctual than saying, "Don't be late". Use positive wording while writing. Journalist Harold Evans urges writers to express even a negative idea in a positive form.[2] The idea will stick better. Here are some examples.

Negative	Positive
Make sure the launch does not face any problems.	Make sure the launch happens smoothly.
We don't want the plan to fail.	We want the plan to succeed.
This bug does not allow the user to check their profile.	This bug stops the user from checking their profile.
We have decided not to proceed with the partnership.	We have decided to terminate the partnership.

Never ask a question using a negative. You'll make the answer difficult to decipher. Consider this question:

Isn't anybody looking into the issue?

Suppose someone replies with a one-word answer: Yes or No. Either answer can be interpreted in two different ways.

> No. That's not the case. Someone is looking into the issue.
>
> or
>
> No. No one is looking into the issue.

> Yes. That's right. Nobody is looking into the issue.
>
> or
>
> Yes. Someone is looking into the issue.

The Yes or No makes no sense without more information. Needless to say, if you're ever asked a negatively worded question, give a longer reply than the one-word Yes or No.

Avoid double negatives. Double negatives are difficult to read and easy to misunderstand. They force the reader to flip each negative to understand it's meaning. Here's one such sentence:

> The team is not confident that they will not miss the date.

Did your head spin for a moment? Are you sure what the team is saying? Will they meet the date or miss it? Now lose the negatives and watch the meaning become clear.

> The team is concerned that they might miss the date.

The below negatives might sound cool in a movie, but they fall flat in an email. The dialogue writers were trying to build character, not convey clarity. You aren't writing a screenplay, so don't get into character.

Negative: I don't think we have no problem.
Positive: We have a problem.

Negative: It's not nothing that's going wrong.
Positive: Something is wrong.

This doesn't mean you should ditch the word *don't.* Negatives *are* useful when you want to stop something. Just know the difference. Use positives to encourage action, and negatives to prevent it.

Consider the below sentence:

Don't get distracted from the meeting and work on the escalation.

Let's use brackets to understand how two people can interpret it in two different ways. The first interpretation is:

(Don't get distracted from the meeting) and (work on the escalation).

In other words, you are asking them to do both: not get distracted from the meeting, and also work on the escalation.

The second interpretation is:

Don't (get distracted from the meeting and work on the escalation).

This could have been better conveyed as:

Focus on the meeting. Don't get distracted by the escalation.

Keep it positive. Tell the reader what is there rather than what isn't.

Spell it right

A spelling mistake can cost you marks in school. At work, it'll cost you respect. Use a spell check. It's a free insurance for your credibility. Certain words, however, can go wrong even after applying spell checks.

They go wrong not because you get the spelling wrong. The spelling is right, but the word itself is wrong. There are several pairs of words that sound and even look similar, but they mean different things. Let's take an example.

except – expect

- I expect to meet all team members today.
- I met all team members except Aditi.

This is a deceptive pair of words. I am looking at them side by side, and I still have to squint to tell them apart. The confusion can be explained by how our brains process the written language.

When we are reading, our brain sees the word as a picture, not as a group of letters. That's why most of us can read misspelled words as long as the first and last letters are in place.[9]

farther – further

Use *farther* when referring to distance, and *further* when you want to say more.[10]

- The meeting room is farther down the hall.
- Let's discuss this further in the next meeting.

compliment – complement

Compliment means giving praise, whereas *complement* means improving something or making it complete.

- The CFO complimented the team on exceeding their targets.
- Strawberries and cream complement each other well.

weather – whether

- The weather is bright and cheerful today.
- I don't know whether I'll get promoted.

The list of such words is not limited to those that start and end with the same letters.

effect – affect

Effect is a noun, whereas *affect* is a verb.[11]

- You will see the effect of the new process.
- The new process will affect everyone.

morale – moral

- Employee morale goes high or low.
- The moral of the story is: honesty is the best policy.

principle – principal

- Clarity is a matter of principle.
- The school principal met the students.

quiet – quite

- Shh! Keep quiet.
- That's quite interesting.

Here are more words to keep an eye on.

piece – peace	foul – fowl
bear – bare	pair – pear
their – there	plane – plain
then – than	knew – new
right – write	alter – altar
site – cite	waste – waist
here – hear	led – lead
hole – whole	stationary – stationery
complaint – compliant	deprecate – depreciate

Cut unnecessary words

We often add unnecessary words when speaking. While they go unnoticed in conversations, they make your writing feel heavy. The sentence grows heavier with every extra word and slowly wears out the reader.

We are in the process of testing the software.

Here's a tip. Every time you write *in the process of*, slap yourself hard (I just did), and then rewrite the sentence without it. The meaning will remain unchanged.

We are testing the software.

Let's look at more examples.

We will meet up with the vendor tomorrow.

The words *up with* are extra. You could have just as well said:

We will meet the vendor tomorrow.

Here's another sentence.

They are leaders in the field of AI.

You could have simply said:

They are leaders in AI.

Read the below sentences twice, first with the underlined word and then without it. You'll notice that the meaning remains unchanged.

They worked hard in order to meet the date. Let's consult with an expert. Please check up on the status. Let's divide up the tasks. Let's test out the product in a small market. The issue was resolved by means of changing a configuration.

Here are some more examples:

call up	lift up
plan ahead	collaborate together
split up	merge together
each and every	revert back

Sometimes, you can replace a long set of words with just one word. Here are some examples.

The stock crashed *due to the fact that* the merger fell apart. The stock crashed *because* the merger fell apart.

Let's *make an effort* to get along. Let's *try* to get along.

In the event that the power fails, the backup will kick in. *If* the power fails, the backup will kick in.

Here are more such words with their shorter replacement.

Long	Short
in connection with	about
with regard to	about
in respect of	about
for the purpose of	to
has the ability to	can
subsequent to	after
prior to	before
as a result of	because

Cut the extra words and your message will instantly feel tighter and sharper.

Avoid clichés

Avoid clichés like 'low-hanging fruit' and 'think outside the box'. Clichés tell people that you have nothing original to say. They make you sound plain and average like the million other people who use the same phrase. Aspire to stand out, not be forgotten. [12]

Ask yourself why you're using a certain phrase. Are you expressing a specific tone or meaning, or are you just using it out of habit? If it's not intentional, replace it with a simpler, more direct alternative.

Cliché	Direct
Let's bite the bullet.	Let's do what needs to be done.
This is a blessing in disguise.	It may not look like it, but this is a good thing.
Let's get the ball rolling	Let's get started.
I want you to hit the ground running.	I expect you to start contributing right away.
We're on the right track.	Our approach is working.
Let's go back to the drawing board.	This isn't working. Let's start over.
I'm calling the shots here.	I'm in charge here.
We should run it up the flagpole.	Let's see what others think about this.
Are we on the same page?	Do we agree?

Why didn't you raise a red flag?	Why didn't you warn us?
The ball is in your court.	I look forward to your response.
Don't drop the ball.	Make sure you follow through.

Here are more clichés that infest official communication.

burn the midnight oil	kick things off
keep your eye on the ball	go the extra mile
crunch the numbers	run it up the flagpole
in a nutshell	push the envelope
once in a blue moon	move the needle
win-win situation	think on your feet
raise the bar	beat around the bush
under the radar	up to my neck
game changer	in the loop
quick wins	behind the scenes
bottom line	long story short
pull the trigger	hit the nail on the head
in the driver's seat	put all your eggs in one basket
throw in the towel	at the 11th hour
on the horizon	reinvent the wheel

None of these will make you sound smart. Rather, they'll make you sound common.

Say it right

If you must use your favourite phrase, though, make sure you are using it the right way. In her book *Get a Grip on Your Grammar,* author Kris Spisak observes that the problem with phrases that are part of our everyday life is that often we don't write them the way they should be written.[13]

Declaring, "I could care less," makes you sound ignorant not tenacious. The correct phrase is 'I couldn't care less'. Don't say someone 'did a 360' if they change their opinion. The correct phrase is 'did a 180.' Don't say 'case and point' when closing an argument. The correct phrase is 'case in point'.

Here are more phrases that people get wrong all the time.

Incorrect	Correct
irregardless of	regardless of
all of the sudden	all of a sudden
by in large	by and large
deep-seeded belief	deep-seated belief
for all intensive purposes	for all intents and purposes
one in the same	one and the same
on your toe	on your toes
tow the line	toe the line
mute point	moot point
do diligence	due diligence
nip in the but	nip in the bud
flush out ideas	flesh out ideas

BEYOND WORDS

Sound like a person

Use a conversational tone while writing. Make your readers feel like you're right there in the room talking to them. That doesn't mean you should mimic your talking style and say, "Bro, what's up?" It means let people see you as a person, and not a stream of words.

Don't sound like a legal notice. Avoid an overly formal and official tone. Use a natural tone. It makes your message feel warm and genuine. Communicating is connecting. You won't connect if you sound like, "Your call is important to us."

Sound like a person, not a robot choking on jargon. Here is a comparison.

Jargon speak	Normal speak
Let's connect soon.	Let's talk soon.
Let's touch back later.	Let's talk later.
Let's circle back to this point.	Let's discuss this later.
We should collaborate.	Let's work together.
We must leverage our synergies	Let's work together.
Let's brainstorm.	Let's think.
We should ideate.	Let's think.
We should pivot.	We should try something different.
Streamline our workflows.	Make things simple.

Let's empower the team.	Let's support the team. Help them. Train them. Anything, but empower them.

The goal is to communicate, not show off your vocabulary.

Showing off: To enhance cross-functional synergy and team cohesion, we propose a strategically curated off-site engagement initiative in an alternative environment. **Normal:** Let's plan a team outing.

Impersonal: In recognition of your proactive and value-driven contribution, we extend our appreciation for your prompt and impactful assistance. **Heartfelt:** Thank you for your timely help.

Stay away from fancy language. It feels impersonal and disengaging. The more jargon and buzzwords you use, the less human you will sound.

Don't sound like them

While it's important to sound like a person, there are some personalities that are best avoided. They repel your readers and make them want to do the opposite of what you are asking.

You can recognize these personalities based on their go-to phrases.

As-Discussed

He likes to remind you: "Look, this happened." Every email has a passive-aggressive tone and starts with: as discussed, as informed, as agreed, as communicated earlier, and as mentioned in my last email.

Know-it-all

He knows and never misses an opportunity to let you know that he knows. His responses are littered with: I know, I knew that, that's so obvious, that's exactly what I had said and needless to say.

Hurry up

Everything is urgent and last-minute, but it's never his fault. You recognize him by: this is super urgent, need it yesterday, what's taking so long, and why does it take so long to?

The Exaggerator

He is a bit of a bully. He amplifies everything, so he's hard to miss. He's always going: It's a disaster, you just lost us the deal, nothing works, the competition's killing us, and do you know what you have done.

Mr. Disappointment

He is never happy. He is impossible to please, and ranting is his thing. He's the one who is: always extremely disappointed, utterly unacceptable, just not done.

Sarcasticman

He thinks he is funny. He is wrong. You can recognize him by: Why am I not surprised, of course it's delayed, you don't say, yeah right, that's just what we needed.

Condescending Guy

He tries to be helpful in a very unhelpful way. He is the one who goes: let me tell you how it works, let me explain, it's really very simple, let me break it down in simple terms.

Please confirm

His motto is: Better be sure than sorry. So, he's always trying to be sure. You know it's him when you read: just to be sure, please confirm, can you confirm. You can never be too sure, can you?

CC

He loves to CC people. He believes that people work only when senior management is watching. His favorite words are CC, FYI, looping in just in case, adding for visibility, and ++.

Embrace any of these personalities, and your readers won't hesitate to put you on mute.

Be professional

Follow social etiquette in an email. Be polite—say please and thank you. Don't be rude or use foul language. Don't tease or make a joke at someone's expense. Don't type things you wouldn't say to someone in person.

This is an email, not a chat. Don't say:

idk wn d mtn is

Use proper English. That means complete words, full sentences, and correct punctuation.

I don't know when the meeting is scheduled.

Adding a :-) after a sentence does not make it sound funny or casual. Stay away from emojis unless you are discussing the company picnic. Delete the Hmm, Oh, Aha, Aahh, Yup, K, Okies, Okey dokey, OMG, ROFL, and ROFs from your email.

Don't use slang in your writing. Here are some professional alternatives to slang.

Slang	Professional
mess up, screw up, goof up	make a mistake
flop, bomb, dud	ineffective
not my jam	not my area of expertise/focus
nailed it	that's right, or good work
slammed	busy or occupied

Don't fake it

Being professional isn't about throwing in words that sound formal or polite. You must show it in every word you write. People can tell when you're putting on a show.

You might think these phrases make you sound professional – they don't.

- If it's not too much of a bother – Are you going to back off if it is a bother?
- If you don't mind – I do mind. Now what?
- I don't mean to be rude, but – Rude statement alert!
- With all due respect – Is something people say when they are about to be disrespectful.

Don't hide behind fake declarations of humility either.

- If I may say so – You are not in school. You don't need permission to speak.
- Correct me if I am wrong – We will correct you if you're wrong. We don't need your permission.
- In my humble opinion – Really?

Be professional, but don't fake it.

Be confident

In professional settings, how you say something matters as much as what you say. Suppose you are the Head of Engineering of a software company, about to launch a new app. Which of these replies do you think is more likely to boost your client's confidence?

I believe we are in good shape. I think we should be okay to go ahead with the launch. We're in good shape and ready to launch.

It is clearly the second reply. Confidence in email writing isn't about being forceful or outspoken. It's about sounding assured in your message. Whenever you make a statement, leave no room for doubt.

If your tone is confident, people are more likely to trust your judgment and take your message seriously. Hesitant-sounding words like *I think*, *maybe*, or *probably* dilute your message and make you sound unsure even when you know what you're doing.

Read each of the below lines twice, first with the underlined word and then without.

I <u>just</u> want to confirm the time. This is <u>actually</u> a good plan. <u>Maybe</u> we should try something different. I <u>kind of</u> see things <u>a bit</u> differently. This is <u>basically</u> the same approach we used before. We <u>sort of</u> need to reconsider our strategy. That's <u>pretty much</u> what I was thinking.

The meaning didn't change, but the lines sounded more assertive without the filler words. Filler words weaken your writing and make you sound hesitant and less confident.

A direct and confident email builds credibility and authority. It leaves a lasting impression and in the long run, establishes you as someone worth listening to.

A word of caution. Show confidence, only if it's real. If you feel the need to say, "I might be wrong", it's best to do your homework before speaking. Also, if you really think your opinion is worth "two cents", then you should keep quiet.

Don't start your sentences with these words.

I think	I believe
I feel like	It seems
It might be that	I guess
Maybe we could	Maybe we should
I'm not sure, but	I'm sorry, but
I could be wrong, but	Just wanted to
Perhaps we can	If I'm not wrong
I was wondering if	This may not be right, but
Sorry to intervene, but	This might be a stupid question
I'm not an expert, but	I apologize in advance

Throw away these filler words, and your message will grow in confidence.

sort of	perhaps
hopefully	a bit
possibly	probably
maybe	mostly
slightly	relatively
generally	typically
actually	virtually
honestly	really
like	essentially
somewhat	supposedly
literally	arguably

Write with conviction, and let clarity do the rest.

Be considerate

I had a colleague—I'll call him Usain Bolt (Not the sprinter). Usain was always in a hurry. He would send an email and dash to my cubicle at breakneck speed. Panting and gasping, he'd announce, "I just sent you an email. Please check it urgently!"

Often, Usain would reach before the email did. I would glance at my screen, feign a frown, and ask, "What email?" Then we would wait, me sipping coffee and Usain standing there like a fish out of water, eyes glued to my inbox.

After what would seem like a lifetime (to Usain), my inbox would finally ping, and Usain would release his breath and me. People bond over different things. We bonded over waiting for his emails.

It's not life-and-death

Every email can't be important, critical, or urgent. Give people the time and space to reply. If it's really an emergency, pick up the phone.

Give them time

Be reasonable with deadlines. Keep making unreasonable demands, and your colleagues will stop taking your deadlines seriously.

Don't be a jerk

Be sensitive about what you write. Don't write a biting email and close it with, "Have a great day."

A little empathy can go a long way in fostering understanding and goodwill.

Write with feelings

Emails have feelings. When you hit the Send button, you don't just share information, you share feelings too. It is often the feelings that decide the response, and not the words.

When reading an email, your eyes read the words but the mind looks for emotions. If it doesn't find any, it fills in emotions of its own—the ones it is already feeling. That's when things start going wrong.

On a bad day, even the simplest line can sound curt or sarcastic. Let's take an example. You're replying to a colleague, thanking him for his help. You reply with one word: Thanks.

Now suppose your co-worker is already angry when he opens your email. Your one-word thanks might leave him seething, "I spent a whole day gathering data, and I don't even get a full thank you."

You were trying to show appreciation, but his mood turned it into disappointment. Emails lack non-verbal cues like expressions and tone that we take for granted in face-to-face conversations.

Unless you are careful, this leaves the door open for misunderstanding. The only way to avoid it is to spell out what you feel. Here is one way you could have said thank you:

> Thank you so much for sharing the information. It was just what I needed. I appreciate you taking the time to gather it.

Control your emotions

A clear mind makes for clear emails. Managing your emotions is a big part of writing clear emails.

Stay calm and respectful

Keep your emotions in check. Don't let your anger or frustration seep into your message. Express disappointment professionally, never with hostility.

Avoid Sarcasm and Insults

If you wouldn't say it face-to-face, don't write it. One moment of anger isn't worth damaging a relationship.

Don't bicker

Emails are not the place for arguments. If you're forced into a war of words, be the bigger person and walk away. Remember, it's about getting work done, not winning the argument.

Praise publicly, Criticize privately

Use people's names when you praise them, but their roles when you raise concerns. A compliment without a name rarely touches the heart, while a complaint with a name will wound deeply. Recognize people in public, but address issues in private or in a smaller group.

Own your mistakes

Everyone slips up. If you do slip up, apologize to the affected person. If the mistake was public, it is best to make amends in public.

Choose to respond, not react

Everything has a consequence

You receive an email that makes you furious—that's stimulus. You start typing furiously and shoot out a reply in 56 seconds—that's a reaction. You continue simmering for another 14 seconds before gasping, "What have I done!"—that's consequence.

Everything you do has a consequence. The consequence of a reaction is usually worse than that of a response. When replying to emails, choose to respond, and not react.

Take your time

What stands between reaction and response is time. Don't reply to important emails immediately. Think it through and then respond. Don't write emails when you are angry or frustrated. Walk away and come back when you have cooled off.

While it's important to pause before responding, it's also important to reply on time. Don't ghost people and make them send reminders.

Avoid silly tricks

Don't shout

Contrary to popular perception, you can't shout in an email without attaching an audio file. THIS IS REALLY URGENT makes you sound irritating, not loud.

Don't go overboard

It occasionally helps to highlight a line or two by making it bold or using a different color, but don't overdo it. Don't switch fonts or colours every other line. Don't get too emphatic. Your words won't sound powerful just because you are using three exclamation marks.

Ellipses

An ellipse (...) indicates an incomplete thought or sentence, which is the last thing you want to see in a professional email. Complete your sentences.

It's not that important

Marking every email as important means you don't know what's important and what's not. Or, you have false notions of your own importance. One reminder is okay, five are not. Get the hint—it's not going to happen over email. Pick up the phone and talk to the person.

MAKE YOUR POINT

Just get to it

I would like to start by drawing your attention to the fact that… Did you go to sleep already? If you did, it's my fault, not yours. You are already reading my book. I don't need to tell you that I am going to speak.

Phrases like these are confidence crutches. They are sometimes useful in face-to-face meetings to draw attention or give you time to gather your thoughts. But, they have no place in an email.

Here are some phrases that make your sentence sound slow and boring:

- I'm writing to let you know that – Isn't that the whole point of an email?
- The point I am trying to make is – Oh! You have a point, not the usual ramble.
- To tell you the truth – Good, you finally decided to stop lying.

And some more.

You know what	Let me start by saying
Just so that you know	At the end of the day
The fact of the matter is that	It is important to note that
I wanted to let you know that	I just wanted to say that
What I wanted to say was	The thing is that

You're writing an email, not ushering in a king or a queen. There is no need to announce yourself.

First things first

Start with the bottom line

Say the most important thing first. Get to the point in the very first sentence so that the reader immediately understands the purpose of your message.

Don't bury key information

If you bury key information in the middle or leave it until the end, it might be overlooked. People often skim emails, and if they don't see the most important detail upfront, they might miss it.

Say it first

An email is not a maths theorem where you must prove a point before making it. In fact, it's the opposite—state your point first, and then build the case around it.

If you are asking for help, start with, "I need your help." If you are publishing software test results, start with the result, "I tested the onboarding page, and it's working", and then get into the details.

Shine a bright light on your message, and your readers won't miss it.

Give a context

Don't assume everyone knows what you know. People might not have the same information, or may have forgotten. Help them by giving a context for what you are about to say.

Set the stage

Think of it as setting the stage. You don't need to tell the whole story, but just enough for the reader to keep up with what comes next.

Without the right context, your email can come across as abrupt and vague. Imagine receiving this email:

> What do you think we should do about the hiring problem?

Without a background, you are left guessing, "What hiring problem?" Now, consider this email:

> There are 4 openings in delivery. We have been interviewing for a month without success—candidates are lacking domain knowledge. The vacancies have started impacting our timelines. Do you have any ideas?

Now, you're no longer in the dark. The email gives your enough information to start thinking on the question.

When looping in

Context also helps when addressing someone who was looped in late into a long email thread. It's inconsiderate to expect someone to read through a week-old exchange between five people and then contribute to the topic.

If you are copying a senior leader, don't say:

> Please give your go-ahead on this thread.

Give a brief summary of what the thread is about and then ask for a go-ahead.

> We had a discussion on how to reduce the time taken between testing and deployment. The below thread captures the entire conversation, but the key takeaways are –
>
> 1. Testing and hardware installation can happen in parallel.
> 2. Deployments can move ahead without waiting for defect trend analysis to complete.
>
> All teams agree with the recommendations. We're seeking your go-ahead to proceed.

Giving background shows clarity of thought and respect for your reader. It takes a minute or two to add the missing pieces, but in return you get fewer follow-up questions and faster decisions.

Say it

Kids can't read your mind

I was finishing dinner at the table. My three-year-old was playing behind me, making it hard for me to get up. Not wanting to bump into him, I said, "Son, I want to get up."

He grinned at me and went back to playing with his truck. "I want to get up", I tried again, a bit louder this time. Another smile, more playing. I was about to ask a third time in an even louder voice, when it hit me.

I was trying to get him to move, but I had not *asked* him to move. I changed my words, "Son, please move aside." And like magic, the truck, the child, and the smile, all three moved aside, letting me pass.

Neither can grownups

Aryan was excited about the coming project review. It was his first project as a manager. "Be prepared. Senior management will be there," he reminded his team twice.

The day of the meeting arrived. The team showed up bang on time, dressed immaculately, ready to answer any question. Yet, not one of them came prepared with the slide deck that Aryan expected. How would they know? He hadn't told them.

Don't be subtle

Say exactly what you mean to say. Don't slip it in between the words. Don't leave it unsaid, hoping that it is obvious. Say it, and say it loud and clear. That's the only way to be sure that people will get it.

It's not that obvious

What is obvious to you may not be obvious to others. Don't expect your reader to figure out the implied meaning of your words. Don't say, "The customer is angry," when what you mean is, "They might cancel the deal."

We often shy away from saying what we really want to say out of politeness or even lack of confidence. A newly joined product manager once wrote to me:

> It takes ten days to develop a new feature using our software?

I knew there was more to his question, but I decided to let him ask when he was ready. I replied with a polite, "Yes. It does". In a later conversation, he finally asked me what he really wanted to ask. His question could have been better expressed as:

> I am told it takes 10 days to develop a new feature using our software. Is that so? I think that's too long. How can we shorten it?

Don't leave the most important part of your message unsaid. Say it without leaving any room for doubt. Don't make people read between the lines and guess the meaning of your text. It's not your readers' job to draw it out of you.

Complete your thought

The worst thing that can happen in a murder mystery is not knowing who did it. Closing an email with an unfinished thought is like the power going out just as the detective says, "The killer is…". Don't leave your readers hanging.

Here are some incomplete thoughts that'll leave your readers frustrated and fuming:

> We should probably consider what this means for the rest of the team.
>
> It's clear that things can't continue like this. I think we all know what needs to be done.
>
> Let's not forget what happened the last time we tried this.

What do you want your people to do? Drop to their knees and plead, "Please tell us what happened last time?" Drop the suspense and tell them what they need to know.

Another type of incomplete thought is when you jump from A to C without covering B. Help the reader understand how you arrived at the conclusion. What's obvious to you may not be as obvious to others.

Consider the following statements:

The customer has delayed the launch by one month. This increases the budget by $500.

The customer has delayed the launch by one month, so we need to retain the hardware vendor for another month. This increases the budget by $500.

The first line makes you wonder, "How does a launch delay translate into a budget increase?" The second line, with the missing link filled in, makes the decision sound completely reasonable.

Sometimes A and C are opposite of each other, and might seem illogical without connecting them with an explanation.

Even though Rahul didn't deliver his last project, we are promoting him to senior manager.

This line is sure to raise eyebrows. After all, you are doling out a reward where a consequence seems to be due.

Though his last project wasn't delivered due to external setbacks, Rahul's leadership and initiative stood out. Based on this performance, we are promoting him to senior manager.

Help your readers connect the dots. Make them glide through your thoughts, and not fumble their way across.

Stop rambling

This is rambling.

> You know the changes that we did recently in our processes; it's been a week since we have started implementing them. I have been keeping a close eye on how things are shaping up. After observing this carefully for a week now, there are some things that I see. I'm not sure whether what we are implementing is the optimal methodology of doing it for our systems. I mean, it seems useful and is probably effective in other places, but it seems like something is off in the way we are seeing things take shape over here, and I wanted to let you know that.

This is direct.

> I am concerned about the new process.

Don't ramble. Make your point quickly without burying it in long explanations and needless background. Nobody has the time to sift through paragraphs looking for your main message.

Rambling comes in three forms:

1. Going off-topic

This is when you go off-topic and bring up the new travel policy in a budget review email. Stay on-topic and save your travel plans for another thread.

2. Over-explaining

This is when you over-explain your point. Trust your writing and your reader's ability. If it takes five paragraphs to land your message, email might not be the right medium for the topic.

3. Repeating

There's a couple's joke where the husband says, "If I said I'll do it, I will do it. Don't remind me every six months." I don't know about the husband, but your readers don't need to be told twice.

Here are some examples where the writer didn't know when to stop.

We have fixed all the defects yesterday. There were no bugs left by the time we left for the day. The report is due on Wednesday. So, it's important that we are ready with it by Wednesday. That is why we should aim to wrap it up by this Wednesday.

Rambling dilutes your message and tests your reader's patience. Respect his time and say what you need to say just once.

MAKE AN IMPACT

Frame it correctly

It's a Monday morning. You have checked in with the team and are about to start your day when your inbox pings. It's a status check from the support team.

> Is no one looking into yesterday's issue? The client is getting restless.

If you are like most people, the question will make your blood boil. Unless you have a good amount of restraint, you'll reply with an equally pointed email.

> Of course, we are looking into it. The team spent the weekend working on it. We know how serious this is.

Now imagine if the same email were worded differently.

> The client is getting restless. Who is working on this? I'll appreciate a status update from them.

A simple reframing of the question turned an accusation into a request. The first email made you want to punch the sender in his face, while the second one made you scramble to support him.

The way you frame your words can be the difference between putting people on the defensive and nudging them to help you. When you use the right language, you lower emotional barriers and get faster and more positive responses.

Let's look at some examples:

> The report still isn't ready. You're going to make us late.
>
> **Better framed:** Everything else is done. We'll move ahead once you share the report.

> The task is still not done. When will you do it?
>
> **Better framed:** I see you're working on the task. Let me know if there's anything needed to wrap it up.

> The figures in the report are wrong. This needs to be fixed.
>
> **Better framed:** The figures are different from what we expected. Could you please take another look?

Small shifts like removing accusatory language and softening the tone can dramatically improve how your message is received. This keeps conversations professional, respectful, and solution-focused.

In the following chapters, you'll learn simple ways of framing your sentences so that your emails meet minimal resistance and make the maximum impact.

You vs I

You must have experienced this. You send a harmless message, pointing out a small oversight or giving minor feedback. Nothing harsh or personal, yet you receive a sharp response. A simple statement turns into a standoff.

It's a pattern that is seen across all workplaces. Not because some people are overly sensitive, or because others are being harsh. It's because our words carry far more emotional weight than we realize.

A common source of such tensions are sentences that are framed using the word You. Let's look at a few examples.

You are wrong. You are making a mistake. You showed up unprepared. You didn't reply to my email. You messed up the client pitch.

Chances are that these statements will elicit a biting reply or a cold silence. That's because they focus on the receiver's action or behavior and hence sound accusatory. They put all the ownership on the receiver, who's then left with no option but to defend himself.

Now let's rephrase the same sentences using the word I.

I have a different opinion. I would have done things differently. I thought you'd be more prepared. I'll appreciate a reply to my email. I thought the client didn't receive the pitch well.

The same sentiment, when expressed using an I, sounds less aggressive and more supportive. It shifts the focus from the reader to you, the sender. You are no longer judging the reader's action. You are simply sharing your thoughts and expectations.

"You haven't shared an update" sounds like an accusation, whereas "I'd appreciate an update" explains what you need. Similarly, "You are late" feels like you are pointing fingers, whereas "I'm worried about missing the deadline" expresses genuine concern.

When making a request, pointing an error or giving feedback, use the I instead of You. Let's go deeper into giving feedback in the next chapter.

Giving feedback

Feedback is everywhere at work. Sometimes you're asked for it, sometimes it just slips out. Whether it's carefully prepared or spontaneous, one thing stays the same—how you say it matters just as much as what you say.

We talked about using I instead of You. Another way to make feedback more effective is to avoid labelling things as good or bad. Instead, share what you noticed and how it made you feel. Keep the feedback focused only on observations that the receiver can use to improve.

It also helps to steer clear of criticism or praise. Both are subjective and equally judgmental. Yes, praise sounds better than criticism, but it is still a judgment. Both shift the focus to how you see things. Good feedback isn't about the giver. It's about the receiver.

Praise: That was a great presentation. Good job.

Feedback: I noticed people were paying close attention to your presentation. The way you paused after each point gave them time to grasp such a complex topic.

Criticism: That was a poor presentation.

Feedback: I noticed people were distracted throughout the presentation. I thought they were having a hard time keeping up with your pace.

Criticism: You were careless with the deadline.

Feedback: I saw that the report came in after the deadline. The project manager had to apologize to the client for the delay.

Criticism: You were very distracted in the meeting.

Feedback: I noticed you didn't share your thoughts in the meeting. I was hoping to hear your perspective on the new plan.

Judgement: That was an offensive remark.

Feedback: I noticed a hurt look on his face when you made the remark. He fell silent after that and soon walked out of the meeting.

Feedback isn't about judging someone. It's about helping them see what they might not have noticed. When you stick to observations, you shift the focus from blame or approval to awareness and growth. It takes a bit more thought, but it turns feedback into something people can actually use.

Why vs What

When asking a question, start with the word *What* instead of *Why*. Why questions tend to create defensiveness and cut off connection. What questions, on the other hand, feel more open and supportive.[14]

Many people feel judged when asked Why. They interpret it as a challenge or an implication of wrongdoing. Instead of answering the question or exploring the topic openly, they get defensive and start justifying themselves.

Let's look at a few questions.

Why are you late? Why did you miss the date? Why do you agree with him? Why didn't you finish your homework?

You won't hear the last question in most offices, but it seemed to fit perfectly with the others due to its tone. In fact, all these questions bring up images of your teacher scolding you for something. Now let's ask the same questions using What.

What held you up this morning? What got in the way of meeting the deadline? What makes you agree with him? What stopped you from doing your homework?

Questions starting with 'Why' often feel confrontational, like a show-cause notice, leading to defensiveness. In contrast, 'What' questions feel more curious and understanding, inviting a more open and useful response. People respond better to What than Why.

Let's look at more examples of Why vs What.

Why did the project fall behind schedule? What made the project fall behind schedule?

Why are you struggling with this task? What support do you need to succeed?

Why did you choose this approach? What makes this approach better than others?

Why did the project fail? What could you have done differently to make it succeed?

An intelligent person knows the right question to ask, but a wise person knows how to ask it.

Beware of But

But is a dangerous word. It can flip a sentence on its head. It can turn agreement into disagreement, praise into criticism, and success into failure. Use but carefully.

Imagine you're responding to an email from an eager team member full of bright ideas. You say:

> You make some valid points, but ...

Doesn't matter how you finish the sentence, what he is going to hear is:

> Your points are invalid.

Here are some more examples.

> I agree with what you are saying, but ...
>
> **Translation:** I disagree.

> I love the idea, but ...
>
> **Translation:** I hate the idea.

A close cousin of *but* is *however.*

> You are right that we should follow the recommendations, however …
>
> **Translation:** You are wrong. Let's throw away those stupid recommendations.

Avoid using but when giving feedback or responding to an idea. As soon as you utter it, you negate whatever good things you have said till then. It's as if you are erasing whatever you said before.

Doesn't matter how carefully you choose your next words, the only message people will hear is, "You are wrong!" Nothing productive can happen after that.

If it's a peer or a senior, they'll probably fight back. If it's a subordinate, they'll think twice before sharing their next idea. Either way, you've created a barrier in the relationship for no good reason.

I'm in no way suggesting that you lie or hold back your opinions. I'm saying that what you think is praise may not be received that way, or what you call encouragement might not feel encouraging.

So, what's the solution? There's no single answer, but in such situations, it helps to ask yourself, "What am I trying to achieve?" The answer will lead you to one of the following choices:

Eat your words (for now)

If the purpose is to shower praise, then offer the compliment and save the critique for another time.

> You make a valid point. Let's discuss it in detail in our next meeting.

Separate the two messages

Let's say the initiative was commendable, but the idea was wrong. You should convey both messages in separate sentences.

> I love the initiative. I see technical challenges in what you are proposing, but don't let that stop you from thinking more on this. Do keep the ideas coming in.

Say it the way it is

If you don't like it, say it without hiding behind words.

> I disagree.
> I have a different take on the matter.

It's okay to disagree. It's okay to say no. Just don't feel compelled to sugar-coat it. Say it the way it is.

Please, Thank you and Sorry

We're taught to say Please, Thank you, and Sorry as kids. It's a simple lesson that stays relevant throughout our lives. These three simple words matter just as much in professional communication as they did in kindergarten.

Please opens doors

Please signals respect. It shows you're making a request, not giving an order. It tells people that you're not taking them for granted. Adding please at the start of a sentence costs nothing but adds a lot of goodwill to it.

Please let me know if you have any questions. Could you please do it by noon? Would you please review the document today itself? Can you please confirm your availability?

Thank you strengthens relationships

"Thank you" tells people that you value them. It shows that what they do matters to you, and by extension, they matter to you. But don't just say Thank you and stop. A good thank you has three parts:

1. The thank you.
2. The reason – Thank you for your advice.
3. The impact – It helped me fix the problem.

Thank you for supporting us during yesterday's launch. Your quick help really made a difference.

Those few extra words are the ones that make your gratitude feel real.

Sorry mends broken relationships

Sorry is a powerful word. It has the power to repair what's broken, but only if you mean it. Say sorry simply and sincerely. Don't tiptoe around an apology; say it clearly.

Tiptoeing: I owe you an apology for what I said.

Actual apology: I'm sorry for what I said.

When apologizing, focus on your actions and not the other person's reaction. Let's look at an example.

I'm sorry that you're upset.

This is not an apology. It's an expression of regret. It's like saying, "I feel so bad that you are upset." A genuine apology would have looked like this:

I'm sorry for what I said. I can see how it upset you.

Make it a point to not belittle the other person's experience. How would you feel if the laundry guy tore up your wedding suit and with a polite smile said, "Sorry for the slight inconvenience." So, don't say things like:

Oh! I'm so sorry, but it's not the end of the world, is it? I'm sorry I was rude, but you know you were wrong, right? I'm sorry. Okay? Now let's not make a big deal about this.

It's also important for the apology to sound sincere, so don't make it sound like you are doing someone a favour by apologizing.

Okay, okay. I'm sorry.

And whatever you do, don't ever say the one-word sorry. Explaining what you are sorry for is what makes the apology real.

I'm sorry I let you down. I'm sorry I hurt your feelings. I'm sorry for the delay. I know it impacted your timeline.

A very important aspect of apologizing is owning what you did, so don't ruin it with an excuse.

I'm sorry I missed the deadline, but the testing team didn't approve the release until today. I'm sorry I was late for the meeting, but the traffic was so horrible today.

When you say, "I'm sorry, but…," you undo the apology making it sound like you have no real reason to be sorry. So, don't give excuses. Be sincere, say sorry, say what you are sorry for, and then just stop talking.

Anticipate the questions

Put yourself in the reader's shoes when you give information. Ask what would you have wanted to know after reading this message?

It has been decided that the daily call will be held at 9 am instead of 10.

An obvious question is, "Who decided this?" Another is, "Why?" But let's focus on the first one. If your reader doesn't know who made the decision, he might dismiss the memo and stick to his usual routine.

Tell him who decided it, and he'll think twice before arriving late.

The COO has decided that the daily call will be held at 9 am instead of 10.

Let's review this email interaction.

Question: Is there a problem in the landing page? **Reply:** No. There is no problem, not in the landing page.

You might be tempted to ask, "Is there a problem on a different page?" A less confusing reply would be:

No. There isn't.

When you provide clear answers and give sound reasoning, people are more likely to take it seriously.

Avoid bottlenecks

Inputs and feedback are a part of office life. These dependencies can slow you down when you're left waiting for someone's reply. You send reminders, chase people, and still get no answer. The good news is that you can reduce such bottlenecks by treating requests in two ways.

1. Critical feedback

These are answers you need before you can move forward. If you don't get them, you get stuck. There's little you can do to speed these up. You can follow up more often, escalate to a manager, or set firm deadlines, but you'll still depend on someone else's schedule.

2. Optional feedback

These are comments or ideas that would help, but aren't essential. You should frame these requests or questions such that they don't block your work. Instead of waiting for every bit of feedback, make it clear that you'll move ahead after a specific time.

Here's how your choice of words makes all the difference.

> Please find attached the design document. Please send me your feedback by 4th Aug.

This request puts your reader in a position of power. It implicitly tells them that you won't proceed without their response. If you do go ahead without their feedback, they can question you, "Why didn't you wait for my feedback?"

Here's an alternative:

Please find attached the design document. In case you have feedback, please share it by 4th Aug, because I'll be submitting the document on the 5th Aug.

This request makes it clear that you will submit the document on 5th Aug with or without the reader's feedback. Their feedback is welcome, but not essential for submission. You own the deadline and stay in charge of your calendar.

Here is another example where the first request forces you to wait for a response, while the second one sets you free.

Should we extend the vendor's contract? I plan to extend the vendor's contract on 31st Jan. Let me know if you think otherwise.

Whenever possible, word your requests such that you're not blocked for someone else's reply. Reserve blocking requests only for occasions where they are essential. This way, you'll spend less time chasing people and meet more deadlines, thus making your life smoother.

START WRITING

How to write

Short and clear emails take a longer time to write. It's faster than what you think, but slower than typing furiously and clicking send. Quickly is the enemy of clear. Time will make you quicker, but don't start with that goal.

Here is the process that works for me. It doesn't have to work for you. Try it on for size and tweak it to make it yours. Writing clear emails is not just an aspiration; it's a habit. If you do it enough times, it'll become second nature.

Write without distractions

Write emails in a minimal text editor, never in an email app like Outlook or Apple Mail. Go for a no-frills space without formatting or spell check. Just you and your thoughts.

Then you write. Write without worrying about getting it right. Write down all the thoughts in your head: full sentences, half sentences, phrases, words. Keep writing until you are out of ideas. That's your first draft.

Write multiple drafts

I call the first draft the ugly draft. A few more will follow. The longer the email, more the number of drafts. If you think your first draft is good, you are being lazy. Never send out the first draft.

Read it aloud

After every draft, read what you have written. Reading, after all, is the purpose of an email. Read it out loud, and not in your mind. And, read it fast. Everybody skims through emails. So, that's the speed at which they must understand it.

Listen to your words

Have an imaginary conversation with your reader. Imagine you are talking to them instead of writing. Listen to how your words sound. What feels acceptable to the mind often sounds ridiculous to the ears. Trust your ears.

Revise, Revise, and Revise

Revise after each reading. Ask yourself –

- Does this make sense instantly?
- Does it convey exactly what I want to say?
- Can it be misinterpreted?
- Can I shorten it and still retain the same meaning?
- Would I say this to someone's face?

Take a printout

If the email is too long or too important, print it. Hold the printout in your hand and read it aloud, tapping each word with a pencil. We often skip words while reading, and tapping prevents that. Make corrections as you go.

Final touches

When you feel like you are almost there, transfer the text to your email app. Apply spell checks. Format the text to give the email a clean and finished look. Read aloud one last time, and click send.

Be patient

Clarity takes time

A clear email doesn't happen by accident. It takes effort and patience. You have to slow down, give the email the time it deserves. That's the cost of doing things right.

Writing clear emails means pausing long enough to think. To choose the right words. To make sure your message is easy to understand the first time. That's what respect for your reader looks like in writing.

No bad questions

Be patient with people's questions. Never make anyone feel bad about asking a question. Just because it's obvious to you doesn't mean it's obvious to everyone else. In fact, the more obvious a question, the clearer your reply should be. If the answer is easy, all the more reason to take a moment and write it well.

Value your readers

When you take the time to write clear emails that people understand, people begin to take notice. They feel valued and they value you in return. That alone makes it worth your time. So, take the time and write it right.

Do your homework

Prepare well

The preparation for a good email starts long before you start typing. Writing a good email is much like talking to people. It takes empathy and patience. You must get to know them before you can really connect with them.

Know your readers

The secret to writing clear emails is not just knowing your content, but also understanding your audience. When you anticipate and answer their questions upfront, your message becomes clearer and impactful.

Get familiar with your readers. Take the time to talk to them. Read through past emails and take note of the questions they routinely ask. Address those patterns in your emails, and you'll be on the path to clarity.

Tailor it

Tailor your language to suit your reader. Use words familiar to them. Don't talk in coding terms with a sales executive or use financial jargon with a programmer.

Put yourself in their shoes, and your readers will feel the impact.

When to avoid emails

Imagine your ideal marriage proposal. What would be the perfect setting for it? You'd probably picture it happening at a meaningful place, with you and your partner looking into each other's eyes. You certainly wouldn't imagine proposing over a text or a phone call. Right?

Choose the right medium for your message

The right medium is essential for every message to make its full impact. A wise person understands when to choose email and when to take a more personal approach.

An email is not an alternative to a real conversation. Don't exchange 10 one-liner emails in a space of 5 minutes. If your emails start to look like a WhatsApp chat, it's time to switch to chat or pick up the phone.

Here's an email conversation that should never have been.

Judy sends an email: When is the project review happening?
Jane replies: I don't know.
Judy persists: What's your guess?
Jane: Around the 10th.
Judy: Ok. Do we need to prepare anything different than last time?
Jane: This is silly. Let's get on a call?
Judy: When should I call you?
Jane: When do you have time?
Judy: I have time now. How about you?
[Two minutes later]
Jane: Pick up the phone, Judy. I'm calling you!

Not always the right choice

Here are some situations where an email might not be the most effective option –

1. If you need a decision right now, best pick up the phone.
2. A long discussion, especially involving multiple people.
3. Having an argument.
4. Convincing someone. Convincing people requires really good writing skills. If you must use an email, send it, but follow up with a call.
5. Apologizing. Apologies are best done in person (or over a video call) with eye contact. You may additionally send an email if it needs to be made public.

Choose the right medium and then let clarity do the rest.

Common emails

The emails you write most often will depend on your job. For these recurring situations, having a go-to outline or template saves time and reduces the chance of missing key details. It gives your emails consistency and clarity even when you're in a hurry.

Here are some ready-to-use templates to get you started, each with key points to guide your writing.

Meeting invite

- Time and Place
- Agenda
- Why it's important
- Expectations from each attendee

Deadline change

- Previous deadline vs new deadline.
- Why has it changed?
- What gets reprioritized? Show flexibility.
- Show empathy. Be open to concerns.

Root cause analysis

- Background
- Cause of the issue
- Why things went wrong
- Analysis – Present data and facts

- Resolution – What is the solution
- Timeline
- Why won't it happen again

Responding to an issue

- Acknowledge the problem
    - Summarize your understanding
- Ask questions
    - Understand the impact
    - Ask for relevant data
- Share the next steps
- Set expectations for the next update
- Show empathy all along

Policy update

- What is the update
- Why the change
- Benefits of the change
- Who does it affect
- Who does it not affect
- When does it take effect
- Where to raise questions

Writing emails is no different from other work tasks. It helps to be prepared and organized.

CONCLUSION

For several months after finishing Write Clear Emails, I remained stuck on the question, "Should I add a conclusion or not?" I've always believed in keeping it short. That's why I chose not to write an introductory chapter. I figured you'd rather get to the point than sit through formalities.

By that logic, one part of me said, "You've said what you set out to say. There's nothing more to say." But another part of me lingered, quietly wanting one last good bye. So, I waited for it to speak, and one tranquil afternoon, as I read these pages yet again, its voice found me.

Clarity must come from within you. It begins in your mind, passes through your words, and lands gently in front of your reader. It matters as much to you as it does to them, because clarity is nothing but your true voice.

My hope for this book has always been to set you on the path of finding that true voice—the real you, standing out in a world of eight billion people all clamouring to be heard.

So, find your voice, and let the world hear it. *Write Clear Emails* is my voice, offered to you with honesty and purpose. Now it's your turn. Speak clearly, write boldly, and share yourself with the world. And when you do, you and I, we'll both have succeeded.

ACKNOWLEDGEMENTS

I've always loved reading, but the realization that I also enjoyed writing came much later in my career. Even then, my writing was mostly technical: emails, design documents, and the occasional report. Although I often found myself helping colleagues refine their writing, it never occurred to me to write a book about it.

The credit for planting and nourishing that idea goes to several people I'd like to acknowledge, in no particular order.

Shani Raja, whose online course *Writing with Flair* remains one of the best writing courses I've taken. The course opened my eyes to subtle concepts like ambiguity in writing, use of negatives, rambling, and missing links between thoughts, all of which we've explored in this book.

I owe a lot to Harold Evans and Deirdre McCloskey. I read Evans's *Do I Make Myself Clear?* and McCloskey's *Economical Writing* with the same enthusiasm I had years ago when I first discovered programming and software design.

And finally, Annie Dillard's *The Writing Life* and Larry Brooks' *Story Engineering* awakened in me a deeper urge to not just write, but to write about writing.

While creating this book, I've consciously and unconsciously drawn ideas and inspiration from these writers and teachers. Acknowledging their influence feels like more than a courtesy—an obligation to honour the sparks that helped light my path.

THANK YOU

As I sat alone in my room, door closed, writing draft after draft, I never truly felt alone. For I knew that on the other side of that door waited my first reader—my wife, Purva. For a long time, she was the only person who read these words, carrying them with the same care that I wrote them. She became my reader, my editor, my fiercest critic, and my greatest supporter—all in one.

With endless patience and unwavering focus, she pored over every rewrite and every attempt at clarity. When I faltered, she spoke the truth without hesitation. When I tried to be clever (or worse, funny) and fell flat, she looked into my eyes and said, "I don't get it." And when the weight of doubt pulled me down, she lifted me with quiet strength.

I wrote the book, but she is the one who held it together. Without her, these pages would have never found their way into the world. This book is as much hers as it is mine. Thank you, Purva. Without you, this book would have fallen apart, and so would I.

Many times, while writing this book, doubt would creep in, "Am I really being clear?" In those moments, I would turn to another trusted source—my eight-year-old son, Iyan. I would have him read a line or a paragraph. If he understood it, the line stayed; if he didn't, it was gone. Thank you, my son, for carrying a weight far beyond your years.

A good answer begins with the right question. For me, that question came from my friend and colleague, Savan Vyas. In one of our conversations, he asked for guidance on writing effective emails. I agreed to help, spent some time making a few notes, and within days, we had our first call.

What I thought would be a brief discussion turned into a series of deep and exciting sessions—walking through emails, word by word. Those conversations, and Savan's curious question, planted the very seeds that later grew into this book. Thank you, Savan, for asking the question that started it all.

ABOUT THE AUTHOR

Parag Chitnis is a professional coach and writer. He began his career building software for the defence sector, but soon followed his passion into the world of telecom. Over the next two decades, he designed and developed mobile roaming products that shaped the way we stay connected when we travel. He finds quiet satisfaction in knowing that if you've ever used your phone while travelling across the world, you have probably been touched by his work.

Over time, Parag's passion for building cutting-edge software evolved into a deeper interest in guiding and mentoring the people behind the code. He found greater fulfilment in the high-performing teams he shaped than in the products he shipped. He realized that the next chapter of his career and life wasn't about building more tech—it was about helping people grow. So, he stepped away from the fast pace of tech leadership and reinvented himself as a coach.

Today, Parag is a certified coach and works with individuals to help them grow, think clearly, and communicate better. His coaching is rooted in clarity—of thought and words. He believes that when people think clearly, they make better decisions, build stronger relationships, and lead more fulfilling lives.

Parag is on a mission to make coaching accessible to more people, beyond just the top layers of leadership. His coaching helps a diverse range of people, from working professionals and college students to homemakers, gain clarity and direction in their personal and professional lives.

Parag describes himself as someone in love with words—willing to spend hours choosing the right ones. No wonder when he's not coaching, he turns to writing, a craft he's deeply passionate about. On his blog paragchitnis.com, he shares reflections on communication, work, and the power of clear thinking. He believes clear writing and clear thinking fuel each other and together, help us grow.

REFERENCES

[1] H. Evans and C. Gillan, Essential English for Journalists, Editors and Writers, Revised ed., Pimlico, 2000.

[2] H. Evans, Do I Make Myself Clear?, Little, Brown and Company, 2017.

[3] "The Charge of the Light Brigade," [Online]. Available: https://www.poetryfoundation.org/poems/45319/the-charge-of-the-light-brigade.

[4] E. Johnson, The Handbook of Good English, New York: Facts on file, 1983.

[5] "adst.org," 2016. [Online]. Available: https://adst.org/2016/04/a-u-s-chinese-mid-air-collision-and-the-letter-of-two-sorries/.

[6] "www.merriam-webster.com," [Online]. Available: https://www.merriam-webster.com/wordplay/what-does-smh-mean-shaking-my-head.

[7] S. King, On Writing: A Memoir of the Craft, New York: Scribner, 2000.

[8] S. McLeod, "Simply Psychology," 2023. [Online]. Available: https://www.simplypsychology.org/ironic-process-theory-white-bear-experiment.html.

[9] N. F. b. A. Sabri, "Ability To Read Transposed Letters Word," [Online]. Available: https://www.canadacollege.edu/esl/docs/typoglycemia_final.pdf.

[10] [Online]. Available: https://www.britannica.com/dictionary/eb/qa/what-s-the-difference-between-further-and-farther/.

[11] "www.merriam-webster.com," [Online]. Available: https://www.merriam-webster.com/grammar/affect-vs-effect-usage-difference.

[12] L. Lowndes, How to Talk to Anyone, HarperElement, 2014.

[13] K. Spisak, Get a Grip on Your Grammar, Career Press, 2017.

[14] M. Lasley, V. Kellogg, R. Michaels and S. Brown, Coaching for Transformation: Pathways to Ignite Personal & Social Change, Second ed., Discover Press, 2015.